GIVING BACK

CECILIA MINDEN

Published in the United States of America by Cherry Lake Publishing
Ann Arbor, Michigan
www.cherrylakepublishing.com

Math Education: Dr. Timothy Whiteford, Associate Professor of Education at St. Michael's College
Financial Adviser: Kenneth Klooster, financial adviser at Edward Jones Investments
Reading Adviser: Marla Conn, ReadAbility, Inc.

Photo Credits: © asiseeit/iStock.com, cover, 1, 5; © Marcos Mesa Sam Wordley/Shutterstock Images, 6; © Lisa F. Young/
Shutterstock Images, 9, 21; © Monkey Business Images/Shutterstock Images, 11, 23; © Melinda Millward, 13; ©
mocker_bat/Thinkstock Images, 15; © Creatas/Thinkstock Images, 17; © fstop123/iStock.com, 19; © Oliveshadow/
Shutterstock Images, 25; © FangXiaNuo/iStock.com, 26; © marekuliasz/Shutterstock Images, 29

Library of Congress Cataloging-in-Publication Data

Minden, Cecilia.
    Giving back / Cecilia Minden.
    pages cm. — (Real world math: personal finance)
    Includes index.
    ISBN 978-1-63362-570-9 (hardcover) — ISBN 978-1-63362-750-5 (pdf) — ISBN 978-1-63362-660-7 (pbk.) —
ISBN 978-1-63362-840-3 (ebook)
    1. Children—Charitable contributions—Juvenile literature. 2. Charities—Juvenile literature. I. Title.

    HV41.M483 2016
    361.7—dc23   2014048654

Cherry Lake Publishing would like to acknowledge the work of
the Partnership for 21st Century Skills. Please visit www.p21.org
for more information.

Printed in the United States of America
Corporate Graphics

ABOUT THE AUTHOR

Cecilia Minden, PhD, is an educational consultant and author of many books for children. She is the former director of the Language and Literacy Program at Harvard Graduate School of Education in Cambridge, Massachusetts. She dedicates this book to volunteers everywhere who give so unselfishly of their time, talents, and money.

TABLE OF CONTENTS

CHAPTER 1

What Is Giving Back?

Philanthropy is offering your time, money, or talents to others. The word comes from the Latin term *philanthropia,* which means "love of man." Sharing what we have helps others live healthier and happier lives. Many people also give back because they are **grateful** for what was given to them.

There are many ways to give. Charities are organizations that **sponsor** special needs. For example, the American Red Cross collects donations for disaster relief. It helps victims of floods, fires, and hurricanes.

Most charities have a similar focus. They enlist volunteers to raise money and donate time to support worthy **causes**. It might be collecting money for cancer research or cleaning up roadways.

What do you enjoy doing? How could you turn that into something that will help others?

The ALS ice bucket challenge, which was popular in 2014, raised money for medical research.

"Nothing but net" is a basketball term meaning the basketball goes through a hoop without touching the rim. In 2006, sportswriter Rick Reilly used this term as a play on words. He wrote an article for *Sports Illustrated* challenging readers "to donate at least $10 for the purchase of an anti-**malaria** bed net." Reilly's efforts, along with help from the United Nations Foundation, helped create the Nothing But Nets organization. Malaria is spread by mosquitoes. Nets are an important tool in preventing infection by protecting children while they sleep. Reilly used his talent as a writer to show others the need for action. His words reached many people and inspired them to help.

Whatever the purpose, the goal is to make a difference in the lives of others. In this book, we will explore how to choose the right **charity**, how much to give, and where you can volunteer. You will need your math skills to help you. So grab a calculator, pencil, and pad of paper. Let's begin!

REAL WORLD MATH CHALLENGE

Tithing comes from an Old English word meaning "tenth." It refers to the practice of donating one-tenth of your income. Lucas receives an allowance of $18.00 per month. He earns $13.75 per week at his job. He wants to donate a tenth of his income to an animal shelter.

- How much will Lucas give away this year?

(Turn to page 30 for the answers)

CHAPTER 2

How to Choose a Charity

There are thousands of people and organizations seeking your help. Making the right choice is important. You want to be sure you get behind a cause you believe in. You also want to know that your money is used to support the cause.

Begin by making a list of five things you enjoy doing. Let's say you like to play sports, read, bake, run, and ride your bike. What charities could use those skills? Reading may lead to tutoring young children. Baking might become feeding the homeless. Riding your bike

Working as a tutor without accepting payment is one form of charity.

or running in a race may help to raise money for medical research.

Before you make your final choice, however, you need to do a little research on each organization. Sadly, there are dishonest groups running **scams**. This means they are keeping the money and not funding a charity. Other organizations spend too much money running the charity and not enough on the people they are supposed to help. Charity Navigator (www.charitynavigator.org) is one of several online sources that can help you make a good choice. Charity Navigator ranks charities with a rating system. Spend a bit of time checking out charities before you make your final choice.

After you have checked out charities online, call the organizations, write letters, or send e-mails asking more questions. How much money did they raise last year? How was the money spent? Use your math skills to figure out what percent was actually spent on the cause. CharityWatch suggests that a charity should spend 35 percent or less of its total income on **fund-raising**

Cookies, chocolate bars, and popcorn are all sold by nonprofits to raise money.

Real World Math Challenge

Orange County Health Center collected $847,619 at its annual fund-raiser. The event cost $350,900.

- Did the hospital spend less than 35 percent on fund-raising **expenses**?
- What percent of the profit was spent on the fund-raiser?

(Turn to page 30 for the answers)

expenses. These expenses include rent, utilities, and salaries.

The need for your time, talent, and money is great. Volunteer fire and emergency workers hold events to raise money. Hospitals, churches, and schools all rely on **donors**.

You've narrowed down your list. There are two or three charities you would like to support. In the next two chapters, you will learn how math skills will help you support your favorite charities.

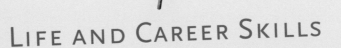

LIFE AND CAREER SKILLS

You should not give to people you don't know who call on the phone, mail a letter, or knock on your door asking for money. Give only to charities you know or to those you can check out yourself.

Making a list of charities will help you choose your favorites.

Do the Math: Raising Money

You need to have money before you can give it away. Start with a **budget**. List your assets, or the money you have. Then list your expenses, or the money you spend. Decide how much you could set aside each month. Creating a budget is an important first step in knowing how much money you can donate.

You might need to give up something. Let's say the cost of a movie ticket and snacks at your local theater is $15.00. You usually go to a movie twice a

Saving just a few dollars a month can really add up.

month. If you skipped snacks at one of the movies, you could save $5.00 a month. That is $5.00 a month, or $60.00 a year, you could donate to others.

Another way to donate to a cause is to get money from others. Be creative. How about organizing a basketball game between students and faculty at your school? You could ask each person who attends to donate $1.00 or a can of food and then give all the donations to a local food pantry.

REAL WORLD MATH CHALLENGE

Mariah's class collected items to fill care packages for soldiers. Mariah is sorting paperback books.

- If she puts 2 books in each care package, how many books will she need to fill 6 dozen packages?

(Turn to page 30 for the answers)

An original idea and a little patience can lead to some very special ways to give back. Many children suffer from medical hair loss. These children have to cope with the emotional trauma associated with baldness. Locks of Love is an organization accepting donations of human hair. Donors grow their hair until there is 10 inches (25.4 centimeters) to cut. Child-size hairpieces or wigs are made from the donated hair. Locks of Love is a great example of how kids can help other kids. More than 80 percent of hair donors for the organization are children.

Something as easy as letting your hair grow long could help improve another child's self-esteem!

Walks, runs, and races are other ways to raise money for charities. Participants ask others to support them by donating money for each mile they will cover. Let's say your uncle agrees to donate $5.00 for every lap you swim. You swim 20 laps. That is a $100.00 donation for swimming in a pool!

A car wash can be a great way to raise money for a good cause and have fun with your friends.

CHAPTER 4

Do the Math: Giving Time

Volunteering your time is another way to give. There are countless organizations that need help from volunteers. Often, finding the time to volunteer is the hardest part. You have responsibilities at home and at school. Use the calendar on your smartphone to help you schedule volunteer time.

Is there a day on your calendar when you have a few spare hours? Weekends and after school are probably your best times. If you can't volunteer on a weekly basis, consider volunteering for a special all-day event. Races and park cleanup days are examples of all-day events.

Cleaning up a park can really benefit a community.

REAL WORLD MATH CHALLENGE

Sophie volunteers at the local soup kitchen with other members of her family. She helps serve food and clean tables. She volunteers 2.5 hours per week. Last year, Sophie volunteered 46 weeks.

- How many hours did she volunteer?

(Turn to page 30 for the answers)

Get yourself organized to volunteer. Think about transportation. How will you get where you need to go? Can your parents take you? Maybe you can carpool with a friend who also wants to volunteer. Think about your safety. Make sure your parents know where you will be volunteering. Also, be sure you check out everything as carefully as you would if you were giving money. Being organized will make it easier for you to make the most of your volunteer time.

Keep in mind that being consistent is as important as the number of hours you spend volunteering. Being consistent means you make a promise to do something and you are there to do it every time. Let's say you volunteer to read every Friday afternoon to an older neighbor with poor eyesight. You need to try your very best to follow through. Your neighbor will look forward to your visits and count on you for help. Be sure to let someone know if you are not able to come by.

Help for elderly neighbors is something many communities need.

Volunteering is the best way to support ideas and causes that are important to you. It is nice to donate money. After all, charities need money to operate. But when you volunteer your time and talent, you get to meet and talk with people who are in need. This is how you will learn that your volunteering has made a difference in their lives.

21ST CENTURY CONTENT

VolunteerMatch is an online tool to help match your skills with a charity. There are special icons to click on for different age levels of volunteers. You can find it at www.volunteermatch.org.

Working in a soup kitchen is a good use of your cooking skills.

What You Get from Giving Back

There are many **benefits** to sharing your time, talents, or money with others. One of the best things about giving back is the opportunity to meet new people. Many people who meet while volunteering become friends for life. Plus, it's exciting to work together on a common goal. It is even more exciting when the goal is met and everyone shares in the satisfaction of a job well done.

Do you enjoy being active and outdoors? Walking or washing animals at a shelter might be a good place for you. Cleaning up a park or roadway is another. Preparing

Compassionate Kids is an organization that teaches children compassion toward Earth, people, and animals.

for and participating in a race will keep you in shape and raise money at the same time.

Perhaps you have a friend or relative who is very sick. Volunteering to raise money for research into his or her disease may give you a better understanding of it. You will also learn how to be a good friend to someone who is fighting the disease.

Reaching out to help others can make you appreciate your own life even more.

When you give back by sharing your talents, you

Habitat for Humanity is a popular organization that builds houses.

might get better at what you know how to do and learn other skills at the same time. Let's say you are volunteering with Habitat for Humanity to build a home. You are also learning teamwork, cooperation, and carpentry skills. Are you volunteering at an arts event? You're learning organizational and social skills. Don't forget that nearly every chance to volunteer is an opportunity to learn responsibility. Others are counting on you for your help.

If you can't volunteer your time, it is a good feeling

knowing that the money you are giving will help others. One person can't cure cancer or save all the victims of a hurricane. Each donated dollar is added to other donated dollars, making it possible for a charity to accomplish its goal.

Pay It Forward, by Catherine Ryan Hyde, tells the story of 12-year-old Trevor McKinney who does favors for three people. When they ask him how they can pay him back, Trevor tells them to pay it forward. He wants them to do a favor for three other people. This starts a human

REAL WORLD MATH CHALLENGE

Kyra and other members of her family set aside $525.00 for charity. They divided the money among 3 groups: an animal shelter, a church, and a public library. The animal shelter received 24 percent and their church received 46 percent.

- What percentage did Kyra's family give to the public library?
- How much is that in dollars?

(Turn to page 30 for the answers)

chain of kind acts. The book itself started a chain reaction when it became a popular movie. From the movie came the Pay It Forward Foundation. The foundation gives students the chance to help find solutions to problems such as violence and pollution.

You, too, can start a human chain of kindness. Who knows how far reaching your good deeds will be. The first step is yours. Start giving back!

21ST CENTURY CONTENT

Some celebrities use their name and influence to bring attention to worthy causes. Oprah Winfrey's Angel Network has received millions of dollars since 2008. The organization uses its money to support a variety of worthy projects around the world. Why do you think people are more willing to support a charity associated with a famous or respected person?

Real World Math Challenge Answers

CHAPTER ONE
Page 7

Lucas will give $93.10 to charity this year.
$18.00 x 12 months = $216.00 from allowance
$13.75 x 52 weeks = $715.00 from work
$216.00 + $715.00 = $931.00 total
$931 x 0.10 = $93.10

CHAPTER TWO
Page 11

No, the charity spent 41% on expenses.
$350,900 ÷ $847,619 = .41398317 = 41%

CHAPTER THREE
Page 16

Mariah will need 144 paperback books to fill all the care packages.
6 dozen = 6 x 12 = 72 care packages
72 x 2 books = 144

CHAPTER FOUR
Page 20

At the end of the year, Sophie had 115 volunteer hours at the local food kitchen.
46 weeks x 2.5 hours = 115

CHAPTER FIVE
Page 27

Kyra gave 30%, or $157.50, to the public library.
24% + 46% = 70% was the total amount given to the other two groups

100% – 70% = 30% was the amount given to the public library
$525.00 x 0.30 = $157.50

FIND OUT MORE

BOOKS

O'Neal, Claire. *Ways to Help in Your Community*. Hockessin, DE: Mitchell Lane Publishers, 2011.

Reusser, Kayleen. *Celebrities Giving Back*. Hockessin, DE: Mitchell Lane Publishers, 2011.

WEB SITES

America's Promise Alliance
www.americaspromise.org
This organization is dedicated to helping build character in young people through service to others and community.

Network for Good
www.networkforgood.org
You can find opportunities to volunteer by searching zip codes, age, and interest areas.

GLOSSARY

benefits (BEN-uh-fits) advantages or positive aspects

budget (BUHJ-it) a plan for how money will be earned, spent, and saved

causes (KAWZ-ez) charitable efforts or organizations

charity (CHEHR-uh-tee) an organization that helps the needy, or a gift to such an organization

donors (DOH-nurz) people or organizations that give money or other gifts

expenses (ik-SPENS-ez) money for a particular job or task

fund-raising (FUHND-rayz-ing) raising money, often for a charitable purpose

grateful (GRATE-fuhl) thankful and appreciative

malaria (muh-LAIR-ee-uh) a serious disease transmitted by infected mosquitoes

scams (SKAMZ) deceptive acts done to make money

sponsor (SPON-sur) to give support and money to a charitable group or organization

INDEX